COZY KITCHEN

Allergy-Friendly Cooking

Jeanette Smerina

For Gary,
I hope you will be my recipe taste-tester for years to come.
Thank you for inspiring me to be creative in the kitchen.

For Claire,
You are the ultimate sous-chef.
Thank you for all of the kitchen assistance, recipe input and book help.

For Andrew,
Your wit and intelligence goes unmatched. So does your appetite!
I always look forward to sharing a meal with you..

I love you all!

Cozy Kitchen Allergy-Friendly Cooking
© 2024 Jeanette Smerina
Copy editing by Cordelia Thomas
Photography by Jeanette and Claire Smerina

ISBN: 979-8-9919600-0-7

UMBRELLA SKY
Media and Production

CONTENTS

Why write a cookbook, Jeanette?

I have a compact kitchen. I also have a husband who discovered he has food intolerance and allergies later in life. Plus, we're an Italian-American family that eats, breathes and sleeps food. These elements separately can make creating meals at home challenging. Put them all together and you have a real conundrum. Not to be deterred, I set out on a path of discovery to make delicious food without soy, gluten and dairy. And I continue to do it all in my roughly 8x8-foot space.

My husband, Gary, was the inspiration for writing this recipe collection. Shh, don't tell him or it might go straight to his head! I'm a professional writer and editor by day, and a domestic food dynamo by night. Alright, maybe I'm exaggerating a bit. I like to cook, and I'd like to think I do it well based on feedback from the people around me.

A few years ago my husband was diagnosed with several food allergies and food intolerances that he had been seemingly living with all of his life. Good food is part of our heritage and the way our family gathers together and connects. Therefore, if he had to start avoiding all of his favorite meals and subsisting only on celery sticks and alfalfa sprouts we'd be collectively heading down a very sad road. (Sorry to all of those who only eat celery sticks and alfalfa sprouts). That's because a family who lives together, dines together in our house. And that meant if Gary had to avoid certain ingredients, the rest of us certainly wouldn't be munching down on said ingredients right in his face (Clandestinely eating them while he isn't around is totally doable, however.) Together with my daughter, Claire, I started modifying recipes so that my husband could still enjoy everything that we normally eat. As I was going along, I started jotting down these recipes and tweaking what worked and what could use improvement.

What's this about a cozy kitchen?

My kitchen is pretty compact. It's not Manhattan studio apartment small, but it's not eat-in, and having a center island would mean bringing in a folding table. I basically have one counter for meal preparation. And don't even get me started on cabinet storage. Real estate agents would call the kitchen "cozy." I know it's just plain small. We were short on time during the home-buying process, and this compact kitchen was a major concession. Seeing as we're foodies, cooking in a relatively tight space is certainly an adventure — particularly when my daughter and I share recipe-making duties. That has grown to be quite often, since we now do more scratch cooking to match my husband's new dietary needs. We're often bumping into each other in the process. I've learned to work with what I have, and that means getting pretty creative. Throughout this book I'll not only share my tips for allergy-friendly eating, but I'll give some pointers on how to maximize the space you have if yours also is a kitchen on the smaller side. Just look for the "steam" symbol beneath many of the recipes.

But I digress ...

Here is why we started switching our cooking and eating habits, and how this cookbook came to be.

Several years ago Gary developed some unusual symptoms that sent him to the doctor for investigation. We were all surprised when he was first diagnosed with Hashimoto's thyroiditis, an autoimmune thyroid condition. Lack of energy, trouble losing weight, difficulty regulating body temperature, changes in mood, skin and hair, and other symptoms can occur with Hashimoto's. The standard treatment is daily medication to regulate hormone levels. This prescription alone didn't resolve all of his symptoms, so we kept digging.

After undergoing an allergy test, we also learned he is allergic to soy. In case you're wondering, soy is in just about everything. Chewing gum, salad dressings, chocolate, many baked goods, and frying oils for chips and crackers contain soy. If you check food labels, soy is probably there. This was perhaps one of the biggest food hurdles to face. Through a process of trial and error, we also learned that foods/beverages with gluten are problematic for him, as well as some dairy products.

Gluten, soy and dairy are evidently foods that cause issues for many people. After some research, we learned that individuals with Hashimoto's and other autoimmune conditions often respond positively to removing gluten, dairy and soy from their diets due to reduce inflammatory responses in the body. We figured we'd give it a try and it worked! Making easy food changes that included skipping soy, dairy and gluten greatly improved how he was feeling. Now it was only a matter of figuring out how to incorporate these dietary changes into the meals we typically enjoy as a family.

Sharing our love of food:

My daughter and I worked together to come up with all of the delicious meals, snacks and more you'll find in this cookbook to fit with my husband's dietary needs so he can eat the meals he loves. There are many other recipes we have, but the ones included are where we started on this journey. We're all in this together and, when we eat as a family, we all enjoy foods we've dubbed, "Gary-safe"! When people eat what I cook now they're surprised that they don't miss the gluten, soy and dairy. In fact, sometimes they, too, feel less "off" after a meal.

I hope if you've been diagnosed with food intolerances/allergies or an autoimmune condition you can enjoy some home cooking that is tasty and helps you feel like the best version of yourself. Always check with a health professional if you'll be making big changes to your diet to ensure they are safe for your own particular situation. Also, if you have a small kitchen like mine, you can rest assured everything in this book can be accomplished in a compact space.

From my cozy kitchen, to yours. Enjoy!

* These recipes are not peanut-/tree-nut free, nor egg-free. Check the ingredients for your dietary needs or allergy. Those with celiac disease should be diligent when buying ingredients to recreate these dishes to avoid all sources of gluten. Also, remember to follow food safety practices during meal creation, including cooking foods to safe internal temperatures.

Appetizers, Small Bites & Sides

Why should the main course get all of the fanfare? It's often those side dishes, little tastes and whatnot, that have my family circling the table for more. If we're not in the mood for a large meal, sometimes I'll just put together an entire spread of small bites and let everyone graze. I may not have started the charcuterie/antipasti trend, but I certainly embrace it.

In this section you'll enjoy some of the supporting characters that often show up in my meals.

Zucchini Bake
Red Pepper Hummus
Eggplant Chips
Sweet Caponata
Creamy Coleslaw
Garlic Smashed Potatoes
Harvest Stuffing
Spinach Risotto
Palm Hearts and Tomato Salad
Tropical Rice

Zucchini Bake

Serves 4 to 6

1 cup gluten-free flour, 1-1 blend

1 tsp baking powder

½ tsp salt

½ tsp ground black pepper

4 eggs

½ cup corn or avocado oil

3 medium zucchini roughly chopped into chunks

1 medium white or yellow onion

½ cup fresh parsley, chopped

¼ cup nutritional yeast

Garlic powder, to taste

Keep only the baking pans and dishes you use repeatedly within reach. This includes your standard options of pie plates and bakeware. Special gear, like springform pans or loaf pans, can be stored higher up or even in other closets of the home and grabbed as needed.

My Zucchini Bake is a variation of "Zucchini Pie," a recipe my mom would make often through the years. I'm not sure where she first discovered it, but it seemed to be a staple among people from her generation, since the dish has popped up at other people's homes from time to time. Her recipe called for a popular pancake and baking mix and shredded mozzarella cheese. But that's not going to work for those eating gluten- and dairy-free. So, I've put my spin on this classic without those ingredients. I find that this makes a good side dish, lunch, or it even can be enjoyed for breakfast because it's more "eggy" than "bready" in consistency. Remember to leave the zucchini skin on for color and texture, not to mention nutrition. Substitute yellow squash if you'd like, or use both!

Preheat oven to 375 F.

1. In a large bowl, mix together the flour, baking powder, salt and ground black pepper. Add the eggs and oil. Mix thoroughly. It will form a thickened batter.

2. Add the zucchini, onion and parsley to the batter mixture. Then season with nutritional yeast and garlic powder.

3. Line a 9-inch pie plate or an 8x8 or 9x9 square baking pan with parchment paper. Pour in the mixture and evenly distribute. Bake in the oven for 30-40 minutes, checking at 30 for doneness. If a toothpick comes out clean, it's ready to enjoy.

Slice and sprinkle with a little extra fresh parsley. Serve hot or at room temperature.

Red Pepper Hummus

Serves 6 to 8

I'm a relatively new convert to the whole hummus game. I've often picked chickpeas out of my salad, but when blended into hummus, I find them to be quite tasty. My husband started requesting hummus in his work lunches because it's flavorful and high in protein, but some of the commercially produced varieties have questionable oils in their makeup. I can control the ingredients by making hummus homemade easily. The great thing about hummus is you can vary the flavors however you see fit. I've made a hummus with ginger and turmeric that was delicious. Red Pepper Hummus below gets an added smoky and sweet kick from roasted red peppers. It's perfect to include as part of a charcuterie platter, and goes well alongside my Sweet Caponata Spread.

2 15.5-ounce cans of chickpeas (garbanzo beans)

3 garlic cloves, chopped

2 lemons, juiced

1 small jar roasted red peppers

3 tablespoons tahini (sesame seed paste)

Drizzle of olive oil

½ cup water

½ cup chopped fresh parsley

1 teaspoon paprika

Salt and pepper to taste

1. Add all ingredients to a food processor or blender. Blend thoroughly until smooth. You may need to scrape down the sides of the appliance and then blend again.

2. Transfer to a serving dish and refrigerate for a few hours to chill. Serve with your favorite gluten-free pitas or gluten-free crackers. Vegetable dippers work, too.

Today they sell multi-use appliances for the kitchen, such as a blender that can process food as well as make smoothies. Investing in one of these tools is a great space-saver.

Eggplant Chips

Serves 6 to 8

1 medium eggplant

2 cups gluten-free breadcrumbs

1 cup cornstarch

2 eggs

2 tablespoons nutritional yeast

1 teaspoon dried Italian seasonings

1 teaspoon garlic powder

Salt and pepper, to taste

Corn or avocado oil for frying

"Italian Salsa"

1 cup cherry or grape tomatoes, diced

3 or 4 fresh basil leaves

Half of one small yellow onion, diced

Salt and pepper, to taste

Small drizzle of olive oil

To say we're eggplant fans would be an understatement. That's why I have two eggplant dishes in this book. When he had to start eating gluten-free, breaded eggplant dishes disappeared from my husband's diet for some time until I started experimenting with the various gluten-free breadcrumbs available. The fried eggplant slices that make up these Eggplant Chips are best served immediately – hot out of the pan. This ensures they'll be crispy. I've found that while the breadcrumbs in this recipe crisp up nicely, once they start to sit, the slices can get a little soft. Serve Eggplant Chips with the fresh "Italian Salsa" that I recommend below, or dip them in hummus, tzatziki or any other favorite dressing.

1. Peel the eggplant and slice into very thin rounds. The thinner the eggplant, the more likely it will crisp up and not get soggy from the oil. Place all slices onto a baking sheet or cutting board and sprinkle with some table salt. Allow to sit for 10 minutes, then pat dry. The salt helps draw out excess moisture and potential bitterness from the eggplant. I jokingly call it, "getting out the poison."

2. Create your breading station: Use a shallow bowl or pie plate and beat the two eggs in it. In another plate or bowl, place the breadcrumbs, cornstarch and all seasonings. Mix to distribute the flavors. Have another dish ready to hold the breaded eggplant slices.

3. Dip the eggplant slices, one by one, into the egg, then into the breadcrumb/cornstarch mix, coating both sides. Place on the dish until ready to fry. In the meantime, heat enough oil in a cast-iron pan or another cooking vessel that will measure about 1 to 1.5 inches deep.

4. When oil is hot, place around 4-5 slices of breaded eggplant in the pan. Wait for first sides to get golden brown, then flip to cook the other sides. Remove slices to a baking sheet or cutting board covered in paper towels to absorb excess oil. Repeat process for all eggplant. Add more oil as needed to the pan to replenish during the frying process.

5. Prepare all of the ingredients for the salsa and put into a bowl. Toss to evenly mix and then serve chilled or room temperature with the chips.

Working as cleanly as possible will help manage the mess in a small area. Cleaning up between the steps of breading and frying the eggplant is important.

Sweet Caponata

Serves 6 to 8

1 medium to large eggplant

¼ cup pitted Sicilian olives

1 red bell pepper, chopped

1 small yellow onion, chopped, or half of a large onion

3 plum tomatoes, diced

2 teaspoons capers

½ cup raisins

2 celery stalks, chopped

¼ cup red wine vinegar

3 tablespoons olive oil

Salt and pepper to taste

¼ cup chopped fresh parsley

Fresh and delicious, caponata is a dish made of eggplant and other regional vegetables. Everyone has his or her spin on the recipe, and like the French ratatouille, it turns relatively inexpensive vegetables into a gourmet dish. Caponata can accompany other dips and spreads on the table as part of Sunday antipasti. Or put it alongside several appetizer type foods for a light dinner ideal when the weather is warm.

1. Peel eggplant and cut into medium cubes. Roughly chop the Sicilian olives. Coat a skillet with the olive oil, and cook the eggplant, olives, pepper, onion, tomatoes, capers, and raisins, for 10-15 minutes on medium heat until soft and browned, stirring frequently. Remove from heat and let cool for 20 minutes.

2. In the meantime, chop the celery and add to a food processor or blender. Add the cooked, cooled eggplant mixture. Pour in the red wine vinegar. Add salt and pepper to taste. Pulse to just blended. You don't want the texture to be too smooth.

3. Transfer to a serving bowl and add the fresh parsley. This is best served at room temperature or only slightly cool. It tastes great on toasted slices of gluten-free bread.

If you'll be making both Eggplant Chips and Sweet Caponata Spread in the same week, cut up your eggplant chunks at the same time you do your slices for the Chips. Store in an air-tight container in the refrigerator until use. It won't matter if the eggplant browns slightly, seeing as it will get soft and golden when mixed with the other Caponata ingredients.

Creamy Coleslaw

Coleslaw is perfectly refreshing and can be the accompaniment to burgers, sandwiches, fried chicken, or whatever you can think of. Coleslaw may not get the same level of attention as potato or macaroni salad at barbecues, but it's certainly my favorite of the three. Coleslaw is another of those dishes that can be made easily at home. Give it a try.

1. In a large mixing bowl, blend mayo, vinegar, seasonings, and sugar.

2. Add in the coleslaw mix and stir to blend together.

3. Transfer to your serving dish, cover with plastic wrap, and let chill in the refrigerator for a few hours before serving.

4. Give a taste test and add a little more vinegar or mayo depending upon preference.

Tip: Some stores carry bags of shredded broccoli slaw, which is equally as tasty in this recipe. It also adds a little extra nutritional value to the recipe. The coleslaw in the photo on the opposite page is made with broccoli slaw.

Serves 6 to 8

1 bag prepared coleslaw mix, which typically contains shredded red and white cabbage and shredded carrots

½ cup avocado oil mayonnaise

¼ cup white vinegar

1 teaspoon garlic powder

2 tablespoons celery seed

½ teaspoon salt

¼ teaspoon pepper

1 teaspoon granulated sugar

Garlic Smashed Potatoes

Serves 4 to 6

2 pounds multicolored, mini potatoes or fingerlings

2 tablespoons olive oil

3 garlic cloves, mashed

1 teaspoon fresh or dried rosemary or thyme

Salt and pepper to taste

Fresh parsley, to garnish

When eating gluten-free, the key is to rely heavily on foods that are naturally free of gluten. Potatoes and rice are starchy sides that certainly meet the criteria. Luckily, finding new ways to prepare foods like potatoes only takes a little experimentation. Smashed Potatoes are a hybrid between a baked potato, a steak fry and mashed potatoes. Even though it's a two-step cooking process, the end result is worth the effort. Plus, you can experience stress relief every time you squeeze down one of those little spuds. Serve these potatoes along with any of your favorite main courses. They're great with steak!

1. Fill a large pot 2/3 full with salted water. Add potatoes.

2. Bring to a boil and cook potatoes until just tender.

3. Drain potatoes and let cool 10 minutes.

4. Drizzle olive oil on a baking sheet. Add potatoes, garlic and rosemary. Toss to coat the potatoes evenly.

5. Using the bottom of a cup, can or meat tenderizer mallet, gently smash down the potatoes until slightly flattened.

6. Place the potatoes under a broiler set to High for 10 minutes or so to brown and crisp up the potatoes.

7. Season while hot with salt and pepper as desired. Top with fresh parsley.

As mentioned, use what you have on hand to smash the potatoes; there's no need to have extra equipment for this task. If the potatoes are cool enough, you can even use the heel of your hand.

Harvest Stuffing

Serves 4 to 6

2 loaves favorite gluten-free sliced bread

1 to 2 apples, peeled

¼ cup raisins

¼ cup dried cranberries

2 cups chicken or vegetable broth

½ cup melted non-dairy butter

2 to 3 fresh sage leaves, chopped

¼ cup chopped fresh parsley

Pinch ground nutmeg

Salt and pepper to taste

Olive oil for brushing

Save counter space by putting the apples, raisins, cranberries, butter, and stock directly into your casserole dish, if desired, rather than a large bowl. Add the bread cubes and toss them right in the dish before cooking.

A good stuffing is a perfect accompaniment to a wide array of dishes. It's of course delicious alongside a roasted turkey, but equally at home with chicken or even beside a pork roast. It could be challenging to find a commercially produced stuffing that is gluten-free, but luckily it's relatively easy to make a homemade version with some basic ingredients. I call this version of stuffing "harvest" because of the inclusion of apples, raisins and cranberries.

1. Cut the bread slices into cubes and place on a cookie sheet. Brush or spray with a very thin coat of olive oil. Preheat oven to 350 F, and place bread cubes to toast for 5-10 minutes until slightly crunchy, being careful not to burn.

2. Peel and slice the apples. Cut into small chunks and place into a large bowl. Add the raisins and cranberries. Then add the toasted bread cubes.

3. Pour the chicken stock and melted butter over the ingredients and toss to evenly distribute. Add the herbs, nutmeg and salt and pepper. Again, mix to distribute.

4. Transfer the mixture to a casserole dish. Return to the oven for another 10 minutes just to warm up. If the stuffing is a tad dry, add a little more stock.

Tip: This stuffing can be customized for any season or meal. For sweeter versions, use berries or peaches in place of the apples, raisins and cranberries. You could even leave out the herbs, replace the stock with apple juice, and turn this into a bread pudding of sorts, served with non-dairy cream on top.

Spinach Risotto

Serves 6 to 8

2 cups arborio rice

32 ounces chicken stock (one standard boxed container)

2 garlic cloves, chopped

1 bag fresh baby spinach leaves

½ bottle dry white wine

3 teaspoons nutritional yeast

1 teaspoon sea salt

2 teaspoons olive oil

2 tablespoons soy-free butter alternative

Fresh parsley to garnish

Risotto is a dish that needs to be watched and tended to often. If your cozy kitchen allows, this is a great time to enlist a "helper" to stir the risotto frequently, or to assist with pouring in the wine or stock.

Risotto is an Italian dish made from cooking starchy, short-grain rice in a liquid until tender. Most people use arborio because it is readily available. Risotto is versatile because it can be modified with many flavors and additions. Add sautéed mushrooms, for example, or swap out the spinach in this dish with peas. When I want to dress up a meal, I'll serve Risotto as a side dish in lieu of another type of rice. It just imparts a little extra "wow" appeal.

1. Heat olive oil in a cast iron skillet or Dutch oven over medium heat.

2. Add chopped garlic and uncooked arborio rice, and mix to coat with oil. Add the butter alternative, and cook until slightly golden.

3. Add one cup of stock, stirring continuously until all liquid is absorbed by the rice.

4. Repeat the process, alternating stock and white wine, until the rice expands and becomes tender and creamy, about 20 minutes.

5. Add baby spinach, and cook until tender and mixed into the rice.

6. Stir in the nutritional yeast and salt. Garnish with parsley.

7. Serve immediately with your favorite main course.

Palm Hearts and Tomato Salad

Salads are a great addition to any meal, but traditional "leafy" salads can sometimes get overdone. When my husband's coworker told him about making salad from palm hearts, I was requested to give it a go. Palm hearts are harvested from the core of certain palm trees. When raw they are crunchy, but stores often sell them marinating in a salty brine. They're reminiscent of a smoother artichoke heart, and are very mild in flavor. That means they won't overwhelm the salad, but will soak up the flavors around them. Palm Hearts and Tomato Salad puts together two refreshing ingredients that are perfect for summer barbecues and other meals.

1. Slice the palm hearts into coins. Don't worry if some unravel, as they tend to do that.

2. Cut each tomato in half, and chop the red onion into pieces.

3. Put these ingredients in a bowl, and add the vinegar and spices. Toss everything to coat and distribute.

4. Add the fresh parsley and toss once more. Serve now or chill in the refrigerator, as it's equally delicious cold or at room temperature.

Makes 1 large salad to share

1 jar (25 ounces) of hearts of palm, or the equivalent of 18-20 sticks of palm hearts

3 cups grape tomatoes

1 small red onion

¼ cup red wine or balsamic vinegar

Fresh parsley, to taste

Dried Italian seasoning, to taste

Save the jar from the palm hearts. If you have any salad leftover, put it back into the jar and slip into the refrigerator for easy storage.

Tropical Rice

Serves 4 to 6

1½ cups jasmine or basmati rice

1½ cups water or chicken broth

1½ cups coconut milk

½ cup chopped fresh, canned or thawed frozen pineapple

½ cup chopped fresh, canned or thawed frozen mango

¼ cup chopped fresh parsley

¼ teaspoon cayenne pepper or red pepper flakes

Salt and pepper to taste

Sprinkle of shredded, dried coconut, if desired

Living in the Northeast means we get our fair share of chilly and gloomy weather. During particularly long stretches of clouds and precipitation, we are often dreaming of warmer climates. I like to create meals that evoke feelings of far-off vacations so that we can imagine we're someplace balmy if only for a short amount of time. Tropical Rice features coconut, pineapple and mango. It can be given a little heat with the addition of the right spices and works great alongside chicken or shrimp tacos. Not all of us are cilantro fans, so fresh parsley brightens up the dish and can be a nice garnish.

1. Place rice in a colander and rinse under cool water. Set aside.

2. Bring water or broth and coconut milk to a boil. Add the washed rice and allow to boil for 5 minutes. Then add in the fruit.

3. Cover and reduce heat, allowing the rice mixture to simmer. Check frequently starting after 10 minutes as the rice may absorb and become tender quite quickly.

4. Once rice is tender and liquid gone, season with the cayenne or red pepper, as well as the salt and pepper. Then add the fresh parsley. Top with shredded coconut if you would like.

5. Serve inside of or along side your tacos or fajitas.

Tip: This also tastes great as a side to a broiled fish, like cod or salmon.

The Main Attraction

Here's where you'll find the main courses I regularly serve up for lunches and dinners. Some are relatively quick meals that are easy for weekdays, and others are the ones my family savors when we do our regular Sunday midday supper.

In my house we all eat the same meal; I don't run a short-order diner out of my cozy kitchen. That is why it was so essential for me to create recipes that we could share together and taste delicious, regardless of whether they're allergy-friendly.

CUBAN SANDWICHES
BEEF STEW
PASTA WITH MEATBALLS
PASTA CARBONARA
BALSAMIC GLAZED STEAK
CHICKEN FRANCESE
HONEY MUSTARD CRUSTED SALMON
GARY'S OWN SAUSAGE & PEPPERS
SOUTHERN CHICKEN BOG
MOM'S MONTE CRISTO

Cuban Sandwiches

Serves 4

4 thin, boneless pork chops (about 1 pound)

4 slices thin deli ham

8 dill pickle slices, like the sandwich topper variety

4 gluten-free hamburger rolls

2 teaspoons of a favorite spice blend, like Goya® Adobo

Spicy brown mustard

2 tablespoons olive oil

Sometimes sandwiches are where it's at for meals. They're not just for lunch either; sandwiches can fit the bill for dinner. I came across Cuban Sandwiches after watching a cooking show on television. It looked like something my family would enjoy as a change in flavors. These whip up fast, and you'll never miss the gluten when you rely on the hearty gluten free hamburger rolls that stores offer.

1. Heat the olive oil in a cast iron skillet over medium heat.

2. Season the pork chops with the adobo style spice blend, and add to the skillet. Cook through, about 10 minutes on each side, or until a thermometer inserted into the pork reads 155 F. Set pork on a cutting board to rest and cool slightly.

3. Slice the pork thinly.

4. Assemble the sandwiches by spreading mustard on both sides of the rolls. Top each with a few slices of the cooked pork, a slice of ham, and two pickle slices.

5. In same skillet you used to cook the pork, place sandwiches over low heat. Press down on the sandwiches with a spatula. You also can use a panini press if you have one.

6. Flip sandwiches, and repeat pressing.

7. When bread is toasted and sandwich is warm, remove.

8. Slice sandwiches in half and serve with roasted corn on the cob, baked potato wedges, or your favorite side dish.

I don't own a panini press, so what I usually do to flatten these sandwiches is stack some heavy cast iron pans on top of the sandwiches and let them sit that way over very low heat. Just lay a piece of foil on the sandwiches, and pile up the heavy pans on top of the foil. You also can use other heavy things you can find.

Tip: If you can eat dairy, add a little cheddar cheese to the sandwiches before pressing and cooking. The cheese helps hold all the ingredients together. Otherwise, try a dairy-free cheddar alternative for a little extra zip.

Beef Stew

Serves 6 to 8

3 pounds chuck roast, cut into ½-inch cubes

2 to 3 tablespoons olive oil

¼ cup gluten-free flour or cornstarch

1 small white onion, sliced

2 cups prepared beef stock (or homemade)

1 cup red wine

4 peeled carrots, cut into thick rounds

6 peeled russet potatoes, cut into chunks

3 teaspoons garlic powder

Salt and pepper to taste

5 to 6 sage leaves

2 tablespoons fresh parsley, chopped

If there's one piece of gear to have in your tiny kitchen, it's a Dutch oven. You can use it on the stovetop or directly in the oven. Many people even make bread in theirs, though I've yet to try it.

Beef and potatoes … is there a more perfect meal? Beef Stew is a hearty dish that can warm up any occasion, particularly when the temperature outside is a tad chilly. What I like about making stew is it only gets better the longer it cooks. Increase the recipe as needed to feed a crowd, or store away the leftovers for another night's meal. The leftovers taste even better. This same recipe easily works by substituting lamb for beef. Many ready-made beef gravies or packets you mix with water contain gluten and soy. That's why I make my own with the help of beef stock and gluten-free flour or cornstarch. The red wine adds a depth of flavor. Choose a Cabernet Sauvignon for your stew and enjoy a glass with the meal when it's served!

1. In a Dutch oven, heat olive oil over medium heat.

2. Thoroughly pat dry chuck cubes with paper towels. Place onion in heated oil and cook 5 minutes, then add beef cubes.

3. Sprinkle meat with the flour or cornstarch to help brown the meat and thicken cooking juices.

4. Cover meat and onions with red wine and beef stock. Bring to boil.

5. Add carrots, potatoes, and sage; stir to mix. Then season generously with salt and pepper and add the garlic powder.

6. Let cook for 10-15 minutes on the stovetop. Preheat oven to 325 F.

7. Cover Dutch oven, remove from stovetop and place in the middle of the preheated oven. Let cook for 2 to 3 hours. Stew is ready when veggies and meat are fork-tender.

8. If stew gravy is not thickened enough, make a slurry of 2 teaspoons gluten-free flour or cornstarch and ½ cup more cool beef stock or red wine. Stir into stew and simmer 5 minutes more.

9. Add salt and pepper to taste. Garnish with fresh herbs to taste. Serve over a bed of white rice, polenta or gluten-free noodles.

Pasta with Meatballs

As an Italian-American family, traditional meals are front and center. A standard dish of pasta with meatballs and marinara sauce is a go-to on many a Sunday afternoon. (It's sauce, not gravy … prove me wrong!) My version of Pasta with Meatballs offers all the flavor of this favorite meal without the uncomfortable, "over-filled" feeling that typically comes with eating a lot of gluten-heavy pasta. While you certainly can purchase a jarred sauce, making it from scratch fills the home with a delicious aroma and it is so easy to do (not to mention more affordable and more practical if you're cautious about ingredients).

Serves 4 to 6

1 pound favorite gluten-free pasta brand, any variety

2 cans (28 oz) whole peeled tomatoes

4 garlic cloves crushed and peeled

1 pound 80/20 chuck beef

1 egg

½ cup gluten-free unseasoned bread-crumbs

Seasonings on hand:

Italian herbs blend

Salt and pepper

Garlic powder

Fresh basil leaves

Fresh parsley, chopped

Olive oil

Nutritional yeast

1. In a large sauce pot, heat 3 tablespoons olive oil until hot. Add garlic cloves and cook until only slightly golden.

2. Add crushed tomatoes, Italian seasoning, garlic powder, salt and pepper, and fresh basil. Bring to a boil.

3. Let boil 20-30 minutes, then reduce heat to simmer for 1 hour or more.

4. To make the meatballs: Place ground chuck in a large bowl. Add breadcrumbs, nutritional yeast, salt, pepper, garlic powder, Italian seasonings to taste, and then the fresh parsley. Add an egg. Mix with hands until blended.

5. Grab about ¼ cup mixture and form into a ball that can fit into the palm of your hand, roughly the size of a clementine. Repeat with all meat and set aside.

6. Heat 3-4 tablespoons olive oil in a large skillet. Add the meatballs and cook, flipping halfway, until browned on the outside. The meatballs will not be completely cooked throughout at this point. Add them to the simmering sauce to cook for an hour or more.

7. In a large pot, bring salted water to a boil. Add your pasta and cook according to package directions until al dente, usually around 8-10 minutes. Drain in a colander.

8. Serve pasta tossed with sauce and two or three meatballs per diner.

Tip: For even moister meatballs, replace the breadcrumbs with gluten-free bread slices. Dampen 2 slices of bread with a little water and allow to sit for 5-10 minutes. Crumble this up in the meat mixture.

Stuffed Pork Chops

Serves 4

4 thick-cut boneless pork chops

¼ cup gluten-free flour or cornstarch

16 oz container chicken stock

2 apples, cored, peeled and chopped

¼ cup dried cranberries or raisins

Salt and pepper to taste

½ teaspoon cinnamon

½ teaspoon nutmeg

3 tablespoons olive oil

2 cups fresh or frozen string beans

If your recipe involves peeling apples, potatoes, carrots, or the like, keep a plastic produce bag handy and line a bowl with it. Peel the produce directly over the bowl. Then grab the bag of the peelings and empty in the garbage (or your garden compost pile). This makes the entire process less messy on your small counter space.

I just love how versatile cooking with pork can be. Since the meat itself is mild in flavor, so many different spice profiles can be used depending upon your mood. In Stuffed Pork Chops, I rely on familiar fall flavors to season the meal. Cinnamon, nutmeg and apples aren't just for your favorite latte. They dress up this dish and give it a sweet and warming touch. Because pork is lean and can dry out if you over-cook it, I prefer to let the chops simmer in chicken stock to keep them moist. That stock will absorb some of the flour or cornstarch you used on the chops and tighten up into a light gravy. If you want a more savory stuffed pork chop, experiment with different fillings, such as chopped garlic and spinach or fresh rosemary and sage. I like serving these pork chops atop a bed of mashed potatoes or Harvest Stuffing (pg 20). Use the remaining chicken stock when whipping up the potatoes for a dairy-free, and lower-fat option.

1. On a cutting board, slice into the middle of each pork chop to create a pocket, without slicing the chop all the way in half.

2. Mix the flour or cornstarch with the spices and salt and pepper in a shallow bowl.

3. Dredge the pork chops through the mixture to coat.

4. Heat olive oil in a skillet over medium heat.

5. Stuff the pork chops with the apples and cranberries/raisins. Use a toothpick or kitchen twine to seal shut.

6. Place chops in pan to sear until golden. Flip and brown on the other side.

7. Reduce heat. Add 1 cup chicken stock to the skillet. Cover and let simmer 30 minutes. Check internal temperature of pork has reached 155 F before serving.

8. Serve with boiled or roasted string beans.

Pasta Carbonara

Serves 4 to 6

4 to 5 ounces diced pancetta (or a thick bacon if you can't find pancetta)

3 garlic cloves, chopped

¼ cup olive oil

Black pepper to taste

½ cup white wine

2 whole eggs, plus 2 egg yolks

1 cup nutritional yeast, plus more for sprinkling

1 teaspoon salt

1 pound gluten-free spaghetti or linguine

Chopped parsley, for garnish

Invest in a collapsible colander to use whenever you drain off the water from pasta or vegetables. It can slide right next to cutting boards and not take up a huge amount of space in your cabinet.

Here's one pasta dish that is a true comfort food. Carbonara is salty and smoky, courtesy of the pancetta in the recipe, which is essentially an Italian bacon. Eggs turn into a velvety sauce for the spaghetti noodles rather than cream. In fact, traditional Carbonara recipes feature no heavy cream or milk at all, despite what the finished dish would have you believe. This is good news for those who avoid dairy, especially as the nutritional yeast provides that cheesy tang without the dairy as well. Be warned … serve sparingly, because this is one filling meal, but oh so worth it for an occasional treat.

1. Heat the olive oil in a skillet over medium heat. Add the garlic and pancetta and cook for 5 minutes. Lower the heat and render for a few minutes more. Add the wine and simmer until reduced slightly. Turn off the heat.

2. Meanwhile, bring pasta water and the salt to a boil. Add the spaghetti and cook until just al dente.

3. In a small bowl, whisk together eggs and yolks and the nutritional yeast.

4. Drain pasta, reserving a cup or more of boiled water.

5. Add the spaghetti to the pancetta pan, and stir to coat. Add the egg mixture, continuing to stir to distribute. Slowly add the reserved pasta water to the pan to temper the eggs and create a sauce. Do not add the water quickly or you can end up with scrambled eggs instead of a velvety coating.

6. If the sauce doesn't thicken, put the pan over low heat again for a few minutes.

7. Serve topped with parsley and extra nutritional yeast.

Balsamic-Glazed Steak

Serves 4 to 6

2 to 3 lbs sirloin, London broil or flank steak

½ red onion, sliced

1 jar roasted red peppers, drained and chopped

1 teaspoon steak seasoning blend (check the label to verify it's gluten-, soy- and dairy-free)

4 tablespoons balsamic vinegar

1 tablespoon olive oil

Balsamic vinegar adds tang and sweetness all at the same time. It's not just something you use over salads. In this recipe it helps add flavor to the steak and could help tenderize it a bit as well. Keep in mind that this skillet version of the sirloin will not come out with a crusty, charred exterior. Rather, it's more of a braised texture. If charred and smoky is your desired result, cook the steak on the grill and whip up a batch of the onions, red peppers and balsamic in a small skillet. Then add them as a garnish to the sirloin when serving.

1. Heat the tablespoon olive oil in a cast iron skillet over medium heat until hot.

2. Add red onion and begin to cook until just tender.

3. Season steak and add to pan. Sear on one side for 5-10 minutes. Then flip and sear on other side.

4. Add roasted red peppers to pan as well as the balsamic vinegar.

5. Reduce the heat to medium-low and let cook, covered, until meat reads 130-135 F (medium rare). Remove cover and simmer for 5 additional minutes to evaporate some of the condensed moisture in the pan.

6. Let the meat rest 5 minutes, then slice and serve.

Tip: Serve reheated steak leftovers on a favorite toasted gluten-free sandwich roll for lunch the next day.

Chicken Francese

Lemon adds a bright flavor to just about any food it touches. It's like putting sunshine into a dish. Perfectly tangy and tart, lemon gives just enough zest to chicken in the creamy gravy that comprises this Chicken Francese dish. The gravy thickens courtesy of the cornstarch, which is a key ingredient to have on hand in a gluten-free kitchen since it's so versatile. Serve Chicken Francese with gluten-free spaghetti or a favorite rice side dish, like my Spinach Risotto.

2 to 3 skinless chicken breasts sliced thinly (Should produce 4-8 slices depending upon thickness)

2 lemons

1 egg

2 cloves garlic, chopped

1 cup dry white wine

½ cup chicken stock

1 cup cornstarch, plus 1 teaspoon

1 teaspoon dried Italian seasonings

3 tablespoons olive oil

Salt and pepper to taste

Fresh parsley for garnish

1. Beat egg with a little water in a bowl to make an egg wash, set aside.

Add cornstarch to a deep dish and season with Italian seasoning, salt and pepper.

2. Dip chicken into egg wash and then dredge through cornstarch to coat both sides. Repeat for all slices.

3. Heat the olive oil in a deep skillet.

4. Add two cloves of chopped garlic, and cook until golden.

5. Then brown the chicken slices on each side until golden, but don't over-cook. Remove from pan and set aside.

6. Mix ½ cup chicken stock with a teaspoon of cornstarch to make a slurry. Add it to the skillet to de-glaze the pan and make a thin gravy. Simmering over low heat. Add more chicken stock as needed to create the gravy.

7. Add 1 cup white wine, salt and pepper, Italian seasoning, and squeezed juice of the two lemons.

8. Return the chicken to the pan, letting simmer, covered, 20 minutes, or until tender and cooked through. Cooking longer won't harm the dish, so you can leave simmering on low while preparing side dishes to go with the meal. Garnish with fresh parsley to finish and serve.

I like making recipes that can be started and finished in minimal number of pots and pans. Here you're browning the chicken in the skillet, and then using the same skillet to make the Francese sauce. I've also tossed peas or string beans right in the simmering chicken for a truly one-skillet meal.

Honey Mustard Crusted Salmon

Serves 4

1½ to 2 pounds salmon fillets (choose what's on sale)

Equal parts brown mustard and honey to equal ¼ cup

1 teaspoon smoked paprika

3 to 4 tablespoons gluten-free breadcrumbs

Growing up I didn't eat a lot of seafood, particularly because my father wasn't a big fish-eater. When I met my husband, I quickly learned that fish was a big thing in his family because his dad and uncles loved to go fishing. It became evident that I'd have to step up my seafood-cooking game. I tend to stick to pan-frying or oven-baking fish when I do make a seafood meal. Because it is full of healthy omega-3 fatty acids that can help reduce inflammation and is also quite filling and tasty, we try to incorporate salmon into our meal plans. Seeing as salmon is a little more "fishy" tasting than white fish like tilapia, haddock or cod, I like to counteract that with an abundance of seasoning. Honey and mustard works well to balance the flavor of salmon.

1. Preheat oven to 400 F and line a baking sheet or pan with parchment paper or aluminum foil.

2. Place the salmon fillets on the parchment, skin-side down.

3. Mix the mustard, honey and paprika together in a small bowl. Brush onto the top of the salmon.

4. Place the salmon in the oven, and cook around 15 minutes until the fish has started to get flaky in texture and is no longer a very deep orange. Sprinkle breadcrumbs over the top, and then turn on the broiler to high setting. Broil another 5 or so minutes to caramelize the honey mustard and bread crumbs. Check that the fish is flaky and cooked through before serving with your favorite side dish.

"Gary's Own" Sausage & Peppers

Serves 4 to 6

16 links of favorite Italian sausage (sweet, hot, flavored)

4 bell peppers in various colors, but primarily red

1 small can of tomato paste

1 small onion, optional

3 tablespoons olive oil

Sausage and peppers is a dish that is often served as street food during the summer or fall at various Italian festivals. It also may be found at carnivals and amusement parks. Traditional sausage and peppers is essentially what the title implies: sausage and peppers mixed with sliced onions. While that combination is perfectly fine, as a family we feel that it serves up a bit oily for our liking — and also that there is room for more flavor improvement. "Gary's Own" Sausage and Peppers recipe was adapted by my husband, who gives it a tangy twist with the addition of tomato paste. Enjoy it all on its own or on a gluten free sandwich roll.

1. Slice the bell peppers into strips, removing the seeds and white pith. Slice the onion, too, if using. In a large skillet, heat olive oil over medium heat. Add the peppers (and onion) and let cook until softened, stirring regularly to prevent over-browning. If the peppers will not soften, continue adding about 1/4 cup of water until the peppers become soft. Remove the peppers from the skillet and set aside.

2. In the same skillet, brown the sausage links until almost cooked through. Then remove the links to a cutting board and cut into roughly 1/2-inch slices. Return the slices to the pan and continue to cook until the sausage is cooked throughout. Add back the peppers and onions, and incorporate the can of tomato paste. Let cook or another 5-10 minutes to blend all flavors together. Season with oregano, salt and pepper, if desired. If the "sauce" is too thick, thin it down with a couple tablespoons of water.

Tip: If you're a fan of spicy, choose spicy sausage links, or sprinkle a little red pepper flakes in while cooking.

If you're smart about the order of cutting up your ingredients, cutting the fresh produce first, you don't need to dirty two cutting boards.

Southern Chicken Bog

Serves 6 to 8

4 to 6 boneless, skinless chicken breasts

5 cups of chicken broth

1 large onion, chopped

3 to 4 stalks of celery, chopped

2 to 3 carrots, sliced

3 cups uncooked white rice, like arborio

½ teaspoon Italian seasoning, or your favorite dried seasoning

1½ teaspoons smoked paprika

2 teaspoons black pepper

2 teaspoons salt

3 tablespoons olive oil

A vacation road trip had our family traveling through the Carolinas. Although slow-cooked barbecue is par for the course when traveling south, I wanted to try something a little different and came across Chicken Bog. Apparently this chicken-and-rice dish is a favorite, particularly in Southern Carolina. What's great about this meal is that it cooks up all in one pot and all of the flavors meld together. Another great thing is that since rice is naturally gluten-free, it's a perfect, hearty meal for the entire family.

1. In a large Dutch oven or stock pot, heat olive oil to shimmering over medium heat. Add the onion, celery and carrots, and cook until slightly softened. Add the chicken and brown slightly on all sides.

2. Add the broth and seasonings and bring to a boil. Cover pot and let simmer over medium heat for 2 hours, or until the chicken can be pulled apart easily. Remove the chicken from the broth. Allow to cool slightly on a cutting board.

3. Shred or cut the cooked chicken into small pieces. Add the chicken back to the Dutch oven and return to a boil. Add the rice. Cover once again, reduce heat to low for a simmer, and then cook for an additional 20 minutes or so until rice is tender and most of the liquid is absorbed. Stir at least once during the rice-cooking process to ensure that nothing is sticking to the bottom.

4. Taste and season with more salt, if necessary. Let the bog rest for about 10 minutes before serving.

Tip: If you are short on time, you can always use leftover chicken or a previously cooked rotisserie chicken in this and reduce the initial cooking time for the chicken. Traditional chicken bog calls for smoked sausage added, but I prefer to go without. Feel free to add bite-sized pieces of cooked smoked sausage if you want.

Mom's Monte Cristo

Serves 4 to 6

8 slices favorite gluten-free bread

8 slices deli ham

8 slices deli turkey

Dijon mustard

2 eggs, beaten

¼ cup dairy-free milk, such as almond

Dairy-free butter alternative for pan-frying

Jar of blueberry or raspberry jam

Powdered sugar, if desired

Keep a serving plate in your microwave. As you cook each individual Monte Cristo, put the hot sandwich on the plate and close the microwave door. It'll keep them warm while you finish up the others. It also helps free up space around your cooking area, and ensures the cooked sandwiches do not become splattered by raw egg mixture. Dunking sandwiches can get messy, for sure.

My family enjoys meals that blur the lines between breakfast, lunch and dinner. Breakfast for dinner is something we enjoy once in a while, and brunch-type foods generally work well for these kinds of meals. While on college tours, I had the opportunity to visit a diner with my son and he ordered a Monte Cristo. It's similar to a Croque Monsieur, but adds another meat to the mix … usually turkey. The best part about this sandwich is that it's dunked into an egg mix and pan-fried just as you would French toast, giving everything an extra-special crunch and flavor. Andrew loved it so much, we had to start making them at home.

1. Lay out 4 slices of the bread on your work surface. Spread a thin layer of jam on each slice. The jam helps balance the saltiness from the deli meats.

2. Add 2 slices of ham and 2 slices of turkey to each slice of bread.

3. Spread more jam on remaining 4 slices of bread and place on top of the meats, jam-side down.

4. Beat egg and almond milk together in a shallow dish that is large enough to accommodate the sandwiches.

5. Heat a slice of butter alternative in a skillet until melted.

6. Slightly compress each sandwich, and then dip one into egg mixture, coating both sides. Promptly remove and put in buttered pan. Cook sandwich for a few minutes on each side, until golden brown and meat is heated through.

7. Repeat the process with the remaining three sandwiches, adding more butter alternative between.

8. Sprinkle warm Monte Cristos with powdered sugar, if desired. Potato salad or coleslaw makes a good accompaniment to this dish.

Sweet Treats

Let's face it, although there have been many strides in allergy-friendly offerings in recent years, consumers often are at the mercy of whatever mass-produced products are available. Not to mention, allergy-friendly items, particularly gluten-free foods, can cost much more than their gluten-containing counterparts. Rather than muddle through over-priced desserts that may not be exactly what you are craving, you can create mouthwatering treats to devour at home or share with others during special events. I think I've touched upon many of the more popular flavors in the recipes you'll find on the next several pages.

ALMOND SPONGE TART
CRUMBLY BLUEBERRY BARS
SNICKERDOODLES
CHOCOLATE BARK
CHEWY ALMOND COOKIES
APPLE COOKIE-CRUST PIE
PEANUT BUTTER CHOCOLATE CHIP COOKIES
PINEAPPLE RIGHT-SIDE UP CUPCAKES
SPOONABLE "BROWNIE MUSH"
EASY PEACH COBBLER

Almond Sponge Tart

Serves 8

1½ cup almond flour

½ cup gluten-free flour, 1-1 blend

¼ cup cornstarch

½ teaspoon salt

¼ teaspoon baking powder

4 large eggs

½ cup sugar

2 teaspoons almond extract

1 teaspoon vanilla extract

¼ cup olive or avocado oil

¼ cup melted non-dairy butter

Finely chopped almonds, to garnish

Powdered sugar, optional

My husband loves the flavor of almond, so you'll see it a couple of times in the recipes I've included. This tart is full of almond flavor due to the inclusion of almond flour, almond extract and chopped almonds on top. It's essentially an almond trifecta! If you desire a tipsy version of this dessert, drizzle a little amaretto liqueur over the tart to soak in before serving.

1. Preheat oven to 325 F.

2. Beat eggs and sugar on medium for 5 minutes, or until they turn pale and become fluffy.

3. Slowly add the rest of the wet ingredients until fully incorporated, and thick and glossy.

4. Sift the gluten free flour, almond flour and cornstarch together in a bowl. Add the salt and baking powder. Then fold the dry ingredients into the wet ones until just mixed.

5. Grease a 9-inch tart or round pan, and line bottom with parchment paper.

6. Pour batter into pan; tap to pop any air pockets that form.

7. Sprinkle top of tart with chopped almonds according to taste.

8. Bake for 30 minutes and check for doneness. Rotate once during baking if not using a convection oven.

9. Cake is done when toothpick comes out clean and cake springs back when pressed. Add a sprinkle of powdered sugar, if desired.

Crumbly Blueberry Bars

There are few things better than fresh blueberries bursting with flavor. When those blueberries are included in dessert their power is multiplied. This crumb-topped treat has a gooey center, and the bars are sweet and crumbly all at the same time.

1. Preheat oven to 350 F. Lightly grease an 8x8 square baking pan with butter alternative or a soy-free oil spray.

2. In a bowl, mix the sugar, flour and salt together. Cut in the 6 tablespoons of dairy-free butter until it forms a crumbly texture. If there aren't enough crumbs, add the 2 additional teaspoons of butter.

3. Press half of the crust mixture into the bottom of the baking pan. Bake for around 10 minutes, or until golden brown. Reserve remaining crumb mixture for topping.

4. Add white vinegar or lemon juice to the almond milk to form a dairy-free buttermilk. Let sit 10 minutes to slightly curdle.

5. Whisk together the eggs, baking powder, "buttermilk", brown sugar, vanilla extract, salt, and flour to form a batter. Then fold in the blueberries gently.

6. Pour batter over the cooked crust in pan. Then sprinkle remaining reserved crumb mixture on top.

7. Bake 40 minutes, and check doneness with a toothpick.

8. Let cool one hour before cutting into squares.

Tip: If desired, serve with a dusting of powdered sugar.

Makes 9-12 bars

Crust and Topping:

6 to 8 tablespoons dairy-free/soy-free butter

1½ cups gluten-free flour, 1-1 blend

½ cup brown sugar

Pinch of salt

Filling:

2 eggs beaten

½ cup brown sugar

1½ cups gluten-free flour, 1-1 blend

1 teaspoon baking powder

1 teaspoon vanilla extract

½ cup almond milk

1 tablespoon white vinegar or lemon juice

3 tablespoons cinnamon

Pinch of salt

1 pint fresh blueberries

Snickerdoodles

Makes 25 to 30
depending on portions

2½ cups gluten-free
flour, 1-1 blend

1 teaspoon cream of
tartar

½ teaspoon baking soda

¼ teaspoon salt

1 cup granulated sugar

½ cup olive oil

2 eggs

1 tablespoon vanilla
extract

3 tablespoons almond
milk

For rolling and coating:

¼ cup granulated sugar
(or colored sugar)

2 tablespoons cinnamon

This is the recipe that took me down a rabbit hole of gluten- soy- and dairy-free desserts. I will admit that during the early days of the pandemic, my daughter and I did our fair share of cooking and baking to keep ourselves busy. It's hard to go wrong with the combination of cinnamon and sugar when baking, which led to trying to recreate popular Snickerdoodle cookies. I've tried this same recipe using all-purpose (gluten-containing) flour and I have to tell you, they taste so much better with the gluten-free flour – lighter and chewier. What's fun about these cookies is you can use colored sugar to customize them for any occasion. Use red for Valentine's Day, green for Christmas, and orange for Halloween, for example.

1. In the bowl of a stand mixer, add the flour, cream of tartar, baking soda, and salt. Mix on low just to combine.

2. In a small bowl or large measuring cup, whisk together oil, eggs sugar and vanilla extract until thickened.

3. Add the egg and sugar mixture to the dry, and mix until just combined. Then add the almond milk and blend once more.

4. Cover and chill dough for 30 minutes or more. Meanwhile, preheat oven to 400 F. Line two cookie sheets with parchment paper or use silicone baking mats.

5. In a shallow bowl, combine sugar and cinnamon. Scoop small balls of the cookie dough (about an inch in diameter) and roll in the cinnamon and sugar mixture. Place each ball 2 inches apart on the cookie sheets. Repeat until all dough is used. The cookies will puff and enlarge while cooking.

6. Press down slightly on all cookie balls to flatten a bit. Bake cookies 8-10 minutes, or until edges of cookies are looking set up.

7. Cool cookies on racks. Store in covered containers for up to one week.

I certainly do not have enough space to keep my stand mixer on the counter 24/7, but I find it such an essential piece of kitchen gear that I've sacrificed room in one of my cabinets for the mixer to reside. Just store all of the mixing attachments right in the mixer bowl. Always use caution lifting one of these mixers, as they can be quite heavy.

Chocolate Bark

Makes 6 ounces

½ cup coconut oil (or cocoa butter wafers; see tip below)

1/3 cup cocoa powder

3 tablespoons pure maple syrup

1 teaspoon vanilla extract

½ teaspoon xanthan gum

¼ cup cornstarch

¼ cup raisins

½ cup chopped nuts of choice (almond, walnut, peanut, etc.)

Scour the shelves of any grocery or convenience store for chocolate and you're bound to find most products, whether dark or milk chocolate, contain a similar ingredient … soy lecithin. This is an emulsifier that helps hold the chocolate together. For those with a soy allergy, that means that most commercially produced chocolate products are going to be off-limits. But everyone deserves a little bite of chocolate from time to time, which is why I just had to come up with a way to create a chocolate treat without the soy. My Chocolate Bark utilizes coconut oil to keep it dairy free, as well as xanthan gum to replace the soy lecithin.

1. In a saucepan, melt coconut oil over low heat.

2. Stir in cocoa powder and whisk to combine.

3. Add maple syrup and simmer 2 minutes. Turn off heat and let cool.

4. Stir in xanthan gum and corn starch. Add vanilla extract and mix thoroughly with whisk.

5. Add raisins and nuts.

6. Line a small baking dish or toaster oven sheet pan (around 6x8 inches) with aluminum foil.

7. Pour chocolate mixture onto foil-covered pan and spread out into a thin sheet.

8. Place pan in freezer for 30 minutes or until chocolate is solid.

9. Remove chocolate bark from foil and break into smaller chunks. Use a meat tenderizer if you're having trouble breaking it up.

10. Store chocolate bark in an air-tight container in the refrigerator.

Tip: After making this chocolate bark several times with coconut oil, I wanted to try to find a way to make homemade chocolate without a coconut flavoring. I discovered you can purchase food grade cocoa butter wafers online. This enables you to make a more authentic chocolate that's creamy and less coconut-forward tasting. Experiment with what you like best.

Chewy Almond Cookies

Makes 20

2 egg whites

¼ teaspoon lemon juice

2½ cups almond flour, sifted to break up the lumps

1½ cups powdered sugar

¼ teaspoon baking powder

Pinch of salt

Zest of half of one lemon

1 teaspoon vanilla extract

1 tablespoon almond extract

Powdered sugar for coating

Sometimes I simply must spread out onto my dining room table to get the job done. Since these cookies have to dry out for a few hours, I move the pans to the table so they're not hogging up precious counter space. This allows me to do my clean-up before baking.

A friend introduced me to an Italian almond-flavored cookie at an event and I fell in love. My version is made entirely with almond flour, so they are naturally gluten-free. When baked the cookies are chewy, sweet and have cracked surfaces that hug the powdered sugar. Plus they're full of delicious almond flavor. If you like French macarons, you're probably going to love these. Here's my spin, which I call, Chewy Almond Cookies.

1. Whip egg whites and lemon juice with a stand mixer until stiff peaks develop.

2. Sift almond flour, powdered sugar, salt, and baking powder together. Fold sifted dry ingredients into the egg whites.

3. Add the extracts and zest, folding until combined. The dough will be very sticky.

4. Line baking sheets with parchment paper or silicone baking mats. Roll portions of dough into balls, about 1 inch in diameter. Then roll each into powdered sugar. Elongate each ball into an oval on the baking sheets. Repeat for all remaining cookie dough.

5. Leave the cookies at room temperature, uncovered, for 1 to 2 hours to let them dry out. Afterwards, preheat oven to 300 F.

6. Gently squeeze opposite ends of the cookies to slightly crack the tops of the sugary shell that developed.

7. Bake cookies for 20 minutes, or until edges have just begun to turn golden. Store covered. Enjoy with coffee or tea .

Apple Cookie-Crust Pie

Makes 1 pie

Nothing says fall is here better than a delicious homestyle pie that includes apples and other favorite flavors. Apple Cookie-Crust Pie packs tart fruit atop a cookie crust with a crumb topping to tempt the taste buds. We all love it warm from the oven.

½ recipe for "Snickerdoodles," see page 58

4 tart apples, peeled, cored and sliced

¼ cup raisins

¼ cup dried cranberries

1 teaspoon cinnamon

1 teaspoon ginger

1 tablespoon vanilla extract

1½ cups gluten-free flour, 1-1 blend

¼ cup light brown sugar

½ cup dairy-free butter

Pinch of salt

1. Preheat oven to 400F.

2. Make snickerdoodle dough and press into the bottom of an 8- or 9-inch pie plate. Bake 10 minutes, or until golden. Remove from oven and let cool.

3. Meanwhile, mix apples, raisins, cranberries, cinnamon, ginger, and vanilla extract together in a bowl. Add mixture to pie plate with cooked crust.

4. Melt dairy-free butter in a microwave-safe container. In a small bowl, mix flour, brown sugar and salt. Add melted butter and stir with a fork to form clumps.

5. Break and sprinkle crumbs over pie filling.

6. Bake at 400 F for 15-20 minutes until crumbs are golden brown and filling is bubbling and tender.

Tip: To make this pie even more delicious, swap out half of the apples for some pears. If you don't like tart apples, substitute a more mild-flavored apple.

Peanut Butter Chocolate Chip Cookies

Makes 12

6 tablespoons (1½ sticks) soy-free, dairy-free butter

1/3 cup granulated sugar

½ cup brown sugar

1 egg

1½ tablespoons vanilla extract

2 cups gluten-free flour, 1-1 blend

¼ cup corn starch

1 teaspoon baking soda

½ teaspoon baking powder

½ teaspoon salt

3 tablespoons all-natural peanut butter

½ cup soy-free chocolate chips

I thoroughly recommend investing in silicone baking mats or parchment paper for cookie baking. Not only does it help prevent your cookies from sticking, it means you often can save time on cleaning up messy cookie sheets.

A popular franchise cookie shop opened up near my home and Claire and I stopped in to try the cookies. Even though they're massive and delicious, I just couldn't wrap my head around spending that much money for cookies so often. Plus, with limited allergy-friendly options, my husband would be missing out. I decided to try my hand at recreating a similar cookie that someone who avoids gluten, soy and dairy could enjoy. These Peanut Butter Chocolate Chip Cookies are soft, sweet and don't last long.

1. Preheat oven to 375 F.

2. In a bowl of a stand mixer or with a handheld blender, cream together butter sticks and the two sugars.

3. Add the egg and vanilla extract, blending until creamy.

4. Add the dry ingredients to the bowl and mix until just blended.

5. Use a cookie scoop or spoon to portion out 12 cookies – six each on parchment-lined cookie sheets.

6. Bake 10-12 minutes, or until cookies start turning golden brown.

7. Let cool on pan for around 15 minutes, then transfer to a cooling rack.

Tip: They now sell soy-free chocolate chips in select locations. I found some on Amazon and in my local supermarket.

Pineapple Right-Side Up Cupcakes

Makes 20

3 cups gluten-free flour, 1-1 blend

1 tablespoon baking powder

½ teaspoon salt

1 cup granulated sugar

3 eggs at room temperature

½ cup corn or avocado oil

1 tablespoon vanilla extract

1 can pineapple rings (10 count), juice reserved and cut into quarters

Brown sugar to garnish

Each year on his birthday my husband requests a pineapple-upside down cake. There's something I find funny about making a cake with a summery type fruit in the middle of winter, but I humor him since it's his birthday after all. Plus it gives us a feeling of sunshine when the weather tends to be gloomy. I figured why not make a similar dessert in bite-sized form that would give him that touch of birthday magic and delicious tropical flavor anytime he desired? Pineapple Right-Side Up Cupcakes are just the thing. If you place the pineapple pieces just right, you end up with cupcakes featuring cute bowties!

1. Preheat oven to 350 F.

2. In a mixing bowl of a stand mixer, add flour, baking powder, salt, and granulated sugar. Mix on low to blend together.

3. Add in the eggs, oil, vanilla extract, and the pineapple juice (it should equal 1 cup of juice). Keep pineapple rings aside.

4. Mix on medium speed until blended, scraping down bowl sides if needed.

5. Spoon batter into muffin tins lined with muffin cups until 2/3 full.

6. Place two quarters of the pineapple ring on top of each cupcake batter. If desired, sprinkle with a pinch of brown sugar.

7. Bake for 20-25 minutes, until cooked through when tested with a toothpick.

8. Cool on a rack.

I prefer to make sure that my kitchen sink and the dishwasher are empty before making any involved recipe. This way I can toss dirty items in the sink as used, and then immediately load up the empty dishwasher after to get everything cleaned up quickly and efficiently. Otherwise my tiny kitchen can get overwhelmed.

Tip: To create a piña colada inspired cupcake, replace half of the pineapple juice with coconut milk or crème of coconut. Then sprinkle a little shredded coconut on top of the cupcakes after they come out of the oven.

Spoonable "Brownie Mush"

Servings vary

½ cup allergy-friendly dark chocolate morsels, such as Enjoy Life brand

1/3 cup avocado oil

1/3 cup almond milk

2 eggs

½ cup packed brown sugar

1 teaspoon vanilla extract

¼ cup gluten-free flour, 1-1 blend

½ cup almond flour

¼ cup cocoa powder

½ teaspoon baking soda

½ teaspoon salt

Devoting one shelf in a pantry or cabinet to baking ingredients can help ensure you grab everything you need for a particular recipe. Stock the basics and you'll be able to make plenty of recipes with a few, standard ingredients.

Who doesn't love rich, chocolate brownies once in a while? After several attempts to get the perfect brownie consistency and flavor, I ended up with a finished product that was double-chocolatey, but so challenging to cut ... even when cooled. Rather than forego flavor for structure, I figured, why fight what I have and grabbed a spoon to dig in!

When your sweet tooth is calling, a spoonful or two of what can only be described as "brownie mush," a hybrid between a brownie and bread pudding, can be just what's needed. It's great all on its own, or add a scoop of a favorite non-dairy whipped cream or ice cream for the ultimate yum.

1. Preheat oven to 325 F. Grease a 9x9-inch square pan with a little avocado oil.

2. In a microwave-safe bowl, melt the chocolate chips in 30-second increments until mostly melted. Stir until all chips are melted.

3. Add the avocado oil, almond milk, eggs, sugar and extract. Mix until everything is well incorporated and the ingredients thicken.

4. Add the dry ingredients and mix into the wet until incorporated.

5. Pour into the prepared baking pan. Set to bake for 12 minutes, or until done when tested. If you use an 8x8 sized pan, increase the cooking time a bit as the batter will be a little thicker and require longer to be done. It is ready when the middle seems just set.

6. Putting a trivet or a towel under the hot pan, set it into the freezer to chill for 20 minutes or so, which helps "fudgify" your dessert, or make it a little more dense and moist. Remove, and allow to cool completely before spooning.

Tip: As with all of my baked goods, I like to use less sugar than one may find in similar recipes. Something that is overly-sweet just isn't palatable to me anymore (although my daughter may disagree). When you do your own baking, experiment with reducing the sugar and you'll likely find that you're not missing that extra sweetness.

Easy Peach Cobbler

Usually I do not need any special reason to make dessert. However, when my daughter's friend gifted us a bunch of orchard-fresh white peaches that started to ripen quickly in my fruit bowl, I figured it best to come up with some way to put them to use pronto. Of course warm peach cobbler came to mind! This recipe for Easy Peach Cobbler is a one-pan treat, so it's great for a cozy kitchen in that you don't have to use a bunch of tools. This is so gooey and delicious right out of the skillet, it's bound to be a family favorite.

Serves 4 to 6

4 cups sliced peaches

¾ cup sugar

Pinch of salt

4 tablespoons soy-free, dairy-free butter

1½ cups gluten-free flour, 1-1 blend

1 cup almond milk

1 egg

2 teaspoons baking powder

Cinnamon to taste

Dairy-free ice cream, optional

1. Preheat oven to 350 F. Peel, core and slice enough peaches to equal roughly 4 cups. Set aside.

2. In a large cast-iron skillet, melt the butter over medium heat on the stovetop. Add the peaches, 1/4 cup sugar and pinch of salt. Let cook for about 5 minutes to soften the peaches and incorporate the flavors. Turn off the burner.

3. In a bowl, mix together the flour, remaining sugar, almond milk, egg, and baking powder to form a batter-like consistency. It will be a bit thicker than pancake batter.

4. Scoop dollops of the batter on top of the peaches in the skillet and then spread to distribute as evenly as possible. Sprinkle with cinnamon.

5. Bake in the preheated oven for around 20 minutes. Check for doneness and leave a little longer if the batter seems too wet.

6. Serve warm with some dairy-free ice cream, if desired.

Tips, Tricks and Products

When you scratch cook the majority of meals it is relatively easy to formulate recipes that fit with your particular dietary needs. Through trial and error, I've narrowed down these go-tos that I lean on in most of my cooking. Feel free to find your own favorites.

Essentials:
• Plain gluten-free breadcrumbs (or Italian seasoned if you can tolerate dairy)
• Soy-free buttery spreads and sticks
• Gluten-free hamburger and hot dog buns
• Gluten-free bread; white or whole wheat slices
• Savory nutritional yeast flakes
• Gluten-free crackers
• One-for-one replacement gluten-free flour containing xanthan gum
• Xanthan gum
• Coconut-almond milk or plain almond milk
• Yeast-friendly gluten free flour
• Gluten-free pasta
• Soy-free dark chocolate morsels
• Corn starch
• Chicken, vegetable and beef stock, for making sauces and gravies
• Italian seasoning blend
• Garlic powder and other spices
• Rice in assorted varieties
• Potatoes
• Balsamic vinegar
• Avocado oil/corn oil
• Olive oil (check the container as some olive oils are not 100-percent pure and are blended with soybean oil)

Cozy Kitchen must-haves:
• Large cast-iron skillet (12-inch)
• Dutch oven
• Nonstick skillet
• Cookie sheets, at least two large and three small
• Spatula
• Wooden spoon
• Rubber spatula
• Ladle
• Stand mixer
• Emulsion blender
• Blender/food processor combination
• Stock pot
• Small pot

Tips & Tricks:
• Stores carry plenty of allergy-friendly options these days, as I've increasingly seen products at national chains and neighborhood supermarkets. Do expect to pay a bit more for gluten-free items, but the investment is well worth it in terms of comfort and health.

• In many of the recipes I use either corn, olive or avocado oil. I try to avoid seed oils as much as possible because there is some research into their negative effects on health, namely having to do with inflammation. Not being a doctor nor a nutritionist, I cannot speak to the accuracy of studies. If you have concerns you may want to speak further with a health professional. However, I've read that corn oil, despite being a seed oil, is perhaps the best of the lot. Avocado oil has a high smoke point, which means it can be used in place of seed oils for pan frying, if desired, and offers similar benefits to olive oil. Olive oil is the GOAT when it comes to oils, and is great for sautéing and using in dressings and some of the baked goods I include because it adds moisture. Keep in mind that most dairy-free butters do use seed oil and olive oil varieties often are blends with vegetable oil, which likely contains soy. Always read all of the labels!

• Gluten-free foods will not last as long as others, probably due to fewer preservatives. Therefore, only make as much as you can eat in one sitting, or promptly freeze leftovers. Look in the freezer or refrigerated section for prepared gluten-free breads, which helps them stay fresh and avoid mold growth.

• Any batter or dough made with gluten-free flour will be stickier than those made with gluten flours. Wet down your utensil or fingers when handling.

• Most gluten-free, one-for-one replacement flours are not designed for use with yeast. You will have to find flours that are specifically formatted to work well with yeast,

• Use xanthan gum sparingly if you add it to any recipes as an emulsifier. Funny story, I used a little too much in a homemade tzatziki sauce once and it gummed it up to a gelatin-like consistency.

• I don't know what I would do without cornstarch. Honestly, I use it so much in my cooking, from making gravies thicker to blending with gluten-free breadcrumbs to help stretch them further to dusting my fingers and work surfaces to help prevent dough from sticking. Luckily it is one of the least expensive products you can buy!

• Getting used to a diet with much less dairy in it has been admittedly tough. It really is hard to replicate the melting factor and flavor of traditional cheese with dairy-free offerings. I usually just skip the cheese and go with other toppings. But there have been great strides in dairy-free yogurts and ice creams made with almond or coconut milk bases. I've also found soy-free, non-dairy whipped toppings that are great to use in place of other whipped toppings for various desserts.

• When entertaining others, unless they have specific food allergies, usually I just serve whatever I've cooked that is likely gluten- soy- and dairy-free. Unless you advertise to guests that something is "different" they usually don't notice it and typically enjoy it nonetheless.

Behind the Scenes

"Cozy Kitchen Allergy-Friendly Cooking" certainly was a labor of love, and a few years in the making. As a writer you always have publishing a book in the back of your head, but somehow life often gets in the way of making it happen. I knew making this cookbook would take a lot of time and energy. But it was worth it to me to try.

Naturally, I first sought out the traditional route of getting a book published by pitching it to notable publishers, including a few I regularly work with through my primary job. Since cookbook production is so labor-intensive, it's hard garnering interest. I also looked into boutique publishers, but they're very selective in the books they choose to back, and also there is a considerable up-front investment involved.

Knowing my work ethic and my skills with writing and creative layout, I decided that I would take the self-publishing route. In this cookbook, 99.9% of what you see was done exclusively by yours truly (with help from my daughter). That includes recipe creation and testing, writing, food staging and photography, book layout and design, marketing, and more. There isn't one page of this cookbook that I haven't touched. The recipes were cooked and then photographed within minutes. A little while later I'd find myself in front of the computer laying everything out.

Seeing this cookbook come to fruition from the earliest stages to this printed copy you hold in your hands is extremely rewarding. I hope you enjoy trying the recipes in this cookbook as much as I enjoyed the entire process of bringing them to you. Those who want to learn more or need guidance on your own ventures can reach me at Umbrella Sky on Facebook or @ umbrellasky517 on Instagram. Or send me an email: umbrellasky517@gmail.com.

I'd also like to call attention to a few other star players who helped make this cookbook a reality.

- *Matthew and Jennifer L. for helping with design and marketing inspiration.*

- *Gary and Gail L. for testing out some of these recipes and offering your honest opinions and support.*

- *Natalie Friscia Pancetti for lending publishing expertise and guidance.*

- *Cordelia Thomas and Laura Larsen for being additional sets of literary eyes.*

- *The rest of my family and friends for your encouragement.*

About the Author

Photo by Claire Smerina

Jeanette Smerina is a feature news writer and editor, and now cookbook designer and author. She produces creative editorial, ad development and other revenue-creation solutions. Jeanette's prior experience includes working as a magazine feature columnist, as well as freelance writer. In 2024, Jeanette launched her own media and production company, Umbrella Sky.

Jeanette resides with her husband, two children, her freckled pup, and a boisterous parakeet. When she isn't clicking away on her Macbook, Jeanette often can be found whipping up delicious recipes for her family, engaging in various crafting projects, watching 80's movies with her daughter, or enjoying the amenities of her coastal suburban town.

Recipe Notes

Recipe Notes

www.ingramcontent.com/pod-product-compliance
Lightning Source LLC
Chambersburg PA
CBHW041123120626

46547CB00019B/2829